A Merry
Yorksl
Christ

CU00691394

compiled by
W.R. Mitchell

DALESMAN

1994

Dalesman Publishing Company
Stable Courtyard, Broughton Hall,
Skipton, North Yorkshire BD 23 3AE

First Published 1994
Copyright Dalesman Publishing

Compiled by **W.R. Mitchell**
Front cover by **Ionicus**

A British Library Cataloguing in Publication
record is available for this book

ISBN 1 85568 082 3

To thi mind - Peace
To thy heart - Joy;
In thine outgoings
Nowt amiss,
To thi home-comings
Happiness.

Contents

Illustrations:

1

The Christmas Spirit

Fred Lawson, the Dales artist whose charming let-
ters and drawings were a feature of old-time
issues of *The Dalesman*, described Christmas as
"the great unknown", adding: "If you decide it will be
a poor Christmas it usually turns out a good one; like
most things it seems to be out of our hands." Arnold
Kellett wrote a poem about Christmas cards which
summed up the seasonal glitter and included this
verse:

But see these sentimental scenes
With bogus yule-logs glowing,
And solemn robins wondering why
For them it's always snowing.

Arnold acknowledged elsewhere in the poem what
most of us think - that Christmas has a magical
aspect. This augments its status as a religious festival
while stopping short of the show-biz glamour and
glitter. I have tried to weave a little magic into this
anthology and at the same time to let the pawky
Yorkshire humour come through.

Yorkshire was almost certainly the home of the first
Christmas festivities to be held in Britain. When, in
521, King Arthur won the Battle of Baddan Hills, he

took up his winter quarters in York, where he kept the Christian festival. The rejoicings, spread over 12 days, had such a strong appeal the idea spread to other parts of the land.

Today's festivities are a mish-mash of ideas old and

new. Christianity tended to absorb pagan ideas, transforming them. The holly's association with Christmas may come from an early belief that the plant's real name was "holy". The crimson berries have long been cherished at Christmas for their decorative effect.

Among Yorkshire birds, only the robin features in folklore and myth more frequently than the wren, which was considered sacred except on St. Stephen's Day (December 26), when it was hunted by the populace. When a wren was slain by village lads, they sang doggerel verses, one version commencing: "The wren, the wren, the King of all birds, on St. Stephen's Day was caught in the furze." The body of the bird was carried from house to house and gifts of money were invited.

A list of the most popular carols would include the Austrian "Silent Night" and the 20th century American "White Christmas", made famous by film star Bing Crosby. The Festival of Nine Lessons and Carols, transmitted by television from King's College, Cambridge, keeps us on the right lines and is the model for scores of such festivals at churches and chapels throughout Yorkshire.

If Christmas celebrations began in York, how appropriate it is that carol services are still held annually by York's ancient guilds in one or other of the several medieval churches still open for worship within the walls of York. In contrast are the Santa Specials organised by some of the railway preservation societies. Through the wizardry of television, we were able to share in a Christmas trip on the Worth Valley Railway, with the participants in Victorian garb and much lively carol singing, both on the platform and in the moving coaches.

T'owd   uns   among   us   remember   spartan

9

Christmases when a stocking at the foot of the bed might contain nothing more than an orange, an apple and some assorted sweets. It was the goose, not the turkey, that graced the majority of Christmas boards.

My own memories of a Yorkshire Christmas are wrapped up with milltown life of the 1930's. As a child venturing forth with a sledge about Christmastime, I would chant: "Ally, ally, aster - Snow, snow faster!" And in those days, the weather clerk often obliged. We seem to have entered a period when winters are milder and summers are cooler than they were. It is not easy to get into the traditional Christmas spirit on a muggy day.

It did not take me long to realise that Father Christmas was the greatest hoax in Christendom - that there were many Father Christmases, some with braces, some with holes in their socks and some, may heaven forgive them, with the stale tang of beer on their breath: and all spitting cotton wool from ill-fitting beards.

Christmas, with its blend of fact and fantasy, its orgy of television programmes we have seen umpteen times before, and the stress laid on good food and drink, helps to break up the long northern winter.

Imbibing freely is, for some, an essential part of the festival. T. Thompson, in one of his Owd Thatcher tales, put into this worthy's mouth the following Christmassy observation: "It's th'only time I sup spirits is Christmas an' New Year, exceptin' Saints Days an' when somebody offers me one. Otherwise, Ah'm abstemious."

Nearer the heart of a traditional Yorkshire Christmas, in spirit and choice of words, is this poem by F. Austin Hyde, who lived at Pickering:

Nobbut a lahtle cottage
That thou's come tae, bonny lad.
Nobbut a poor wold shipherd
That thou'll ha'e tae call thy dad,
Bud thou brings tiv us beath God's blessin',
An' we thenk him we've lived tae lairn
The joy that there was roound a Manger,
When Uor Lord was a lahtle bairn.

Yorkshire common sense is well illustrated by the
story of the farmer's small son (recounted by Mary
Burton) who, having listened to the story of the
Nativity, and hearing there was no room at the inn,
said: "Nay, miss, I blames Joseph - he should-a-
booked."

2

Heart of Yorkshire

Wassailing at York

When it is nearly Christmas, when the tree with its coloured lights goes up once more in St. Helen's Square, and more lamps are lit across Stonegate, and the star of one of our oldest inns shines out in the middle of this so-welcome pedestrian precinct, and when the vergers inside the Minster are beginning to set up the crib - then York seems to gather itself closer together, to become a family of people who really belong to it.

The tourists are all gone, the school parties from all parts of Yorkshire and beyond no longer jostle us along the pavements, the festival crowds are no more, and the Shambles is just another narrow street where we shop and cut through to the market.

Colder winds blow across the Ouse and cassocked clergy and habited nuns bend against the tunnelled force of them across Dean's Park and around Minster Yard. No longer do inquisitive noses press against the windows of my pavement-level dwelling in Minster Court - nosy-parkers of all ages, from France and

Germany, from America and Japan, and from almost every country of the world and from every county in England.

Young noses still press against the window of the renovated tuck shop by St. William's College - little girls and one or two small boys, in the green blazers of the school in the red house just across the way, and Minster Song School boys in their grey flannel suits and scarlet caps.

Any day now we shall hear the carol singers. The verses given below are two, with the refrain, from the "Wassail Song" of the North of England, which gives us a picture of the waits of old time. Another two, says a footnote in the "Oxford Book of Carols" (1928), are not suitable for singing in church, being about the bringing forth of beer, mouldy cheese and some of the Christmas loaf!

The text comes from Husk's "Songs of the Nativity" (1968), where he refers to a Yorkshire copy of the carol in a broadsheet printed in Bradford as late as 1850. The first tune from Yorkshire has been familiarised by Stainer. The second was learnt by Martin Shaw, when he was a boy, from his father, James Shaw. He had often heard it in the streets of Leeds in the 1850's. The Rev. J. I. Horton, of Bradford, remembered it being sung by the Waits in the West Riding as late as around 1913.

Bernard Croft (1980)

We are not daily beggars
That beg from door to door
But we are neighbours' children
Whom you have seen before:

God bless the master of this house
Likewise the mistress too;
And all the little children
That round the table go:

Love and joy come to you,
And to you your wassail too,
And God bless you, and send you
A happy new year.

Rhymester at Malton

As a boy, at the turn of the century, I was greeted or even awakened at Malton each Christmas and New Year by these two "rhymes" or rounds. I believe the custom has quite dried out. Both were given in a sort of sing-song monotone.

Early on Christmas Day, boys whose ages were usually under ten would render:

Wish you a merry Christmas and a happy New Year.
We're all teetotallers and don't drink beer.
A little bit of spice bread, a little bit of cheese,
A glass of cold water, and a penny if you please.
If you haven't a penny, a ha'penny will do.
If you haven't a ha'penny, God bless you.
Please will you give me a Christmas box?

It was the girls' turn early on New Year's Day, and their round went as follows:

Master and Mistress, chuck, chuck, chuck.
Master and Mistress, it's time to get up.

Please will you give me a New Year's gift?

J. Taylor (1960).

An American Visitor

During a Yorkshire tour, the great American writer, Washington Irving, experienced a Victorian Christmas with the Bracebridge family.

The signal for the serving of the family Christmas dinner was the striking of the dresser by the cook, who used a rolling pin. The Parson, friend of the family, said a lengthy, well-worded grace; after which a butler entered the great hall bearing a silver dish, containing an enormous pig's head with a lemon in its mouth, the whole decorated with sprigs of rosemary.

The butler was attended on either side by a servant with a large wax light, and the moment they made an appearance the old harper who was seated on a stool beside the fireplace struck up with a flourish and the first verse of a carol was sung. The table was weighted down with an abundance of good cheer, sirloin of beef, pork and turkeys, with mince pie and plum pudding well represented; but the centre of attraction was a huge pie, magnificently decorated with peacock feathers in imitation of a peacock's tail, which took up a considerable amount of table space.

Washington Irving was informed that this was a pheasant pie; traditionally it ought to have been a peacock pie, but the squire was so fond of his pets and peacocks that he could not bring himself to have one killed and eaten, even in the interests of a genuine old-fashioned Christmas.

The butler next brought in a huge silver vessel

which he placed before the squire, and which was hailed with delight by the company. This was the Wassail Bowl of much renown, the contents of which had been lovingly prepared by the squire himself, being composed of the richest wines, with nutmeg, sugar, toast, ginger and roasted crags. Roasted apples bobbed about on the surface.

Having stirred the beverage, the Squire wished all present a merry Christmas, raised the bowl to his lips, and sent it round the table for each to drink from in the primitive fashion.

Barbara Mather-Green (1957)

The "Magnetic Ray"

In the 1930's, I was a radio service engineer with a firm at Ripon. My area of operation covered a radius of about 10 miles around, including Newby Hall and adjacent cottages. By about 1932, I had acquired a second-hand Jowett two-seater car complete with "dicky seat" for my tools and spares.

It was in this ancient vehicle that I remember calling late one Christmas Eve in response to an S.O.S. plea from Newby Hall to repair their radiogram, which had failed them in the middle of a servants' party. It was a lovely moonlit night, just after a short but heavy rainstorm. I had memories of the three gates I would have to negotiate before arriving at the hall, so I suggested to my young assistant Robert that he accompany me by way of tuition in the art of radio servicing - and gate opening.

Robert was quite eager to come, as he also had memories of the bevy of young and lively servants he

was likely to meet. As it was Christmas Eve, there was the distinct possibility of there being mistletoe about in the Servants' Hall, so we set off post-haste to Newby Hall.

We arrived at the first gate, which was an ordinary five-barred type, and Bob got out of the car and opened it, closing it after me. Then we proceeded across the field to the next one. Here I must explain the system of operation of the next two gates. They were of tubular steel, operated by steel plates let into the surface of the road on either side of them. When a car was driven over the plates, they opened and then closed the gates.

As we approached the second gate, Bob said: "Look

at that great pool of water in front of the gate, and me not having my wellies." I replied: "Don't worry, Bob, I've got a special gadget under the car dash which will open and close the gate without you getting out - it works by magnetic propulsion - just watch." I fiddled under the dash as we approached the gate, having seen that the operating plate was nicely covered by the water from the recent rainstorm.

To Bob's amazement, as we approached (and I drove over the hidden plate) the gate slowly swung open. Then as we drove on through the gateway (and over the second plate) the gate again slowly closed, to Bob's explosive comment: "Well, stone me."

The same operation took place at the next gate which also had large pools of water hiding both operating plates. Bob remained in a state of daze and admiration at the ingenuity of his boss until we reached the hall, where the servants were anxiously awaiting our arrival.

Greetings over - and a welcome glass of His Lordship's sherry - I soon sorted out the trouble with the radiogram. Having retrieved Bob from the group of male-starved young girl servants, we got back into the Jowett and headed for home, full of the Christmas spirit, mince pies and a right mixture of festive wine.

On approaching the first gate, Bob said; "Do your stuff, Jack. I don't think I can get out of the car what with booze and ballet." So I fiddled under the dash as I went forward. Sure enough it worked - the gate swung open and closed after us, and Bob let out a whoop of delight.

The second gate opened as I went over the operating plate but on crossing the closing plate it refused to function. Bob, who had been watching from the rear window, said: "Your gadget has packed up - the gate's still open." So I had a look back after I had stopped the car and noticed that the edges of the plate were faintly showing just about the surrounding water.

I thought, well the game's up. Bob is sure to twig the plate and guess how the whole thing operated. So I confessed that my so-called "Magnetic Ray" was a figment of my imagination, and told Bob to get out and take a running jump at the plate, which would then close the gate.

After some sarcastic remarks, he reluctantly climbed out of the Jowett, took a run at the plate, and with a flying leap landed plum in the middle, only to disappear beneath four cascades of extremely muddy water shooting out of the four edges of the plate!

Happy days, Bob, wherever you are now.

John Payne (1989)

3

Cleveland and the Moors

Preparing for Christmas

If a group of people had suddenly been transported from a desert island to the mining village of New Marske in late December, 80 years ago, they would have known that something very pleasant was about to happen. There was such an atmosphere of festivity that everything seemed touched with magic.

Groups of children, returning home from school, enjoyed the aroma of home-baked bread, cakes and pies, mingled with the smell of roasting meat or ham. Country people prepared for Christmas well before the event and many miners kept fowls or pigs so that a week before the great festival there was a wholesale killing of ducks, chickens and pigs.

There was no inn at the village. A man needing a drink had to walk a mile to Marske, where three inns were to be found. Marske also had an off-licence. The owner would deliver orders of bottled beer or stout at threepence a pint. In summer and autumn, the miners' wives made wine - rhubarb, bramble, elderberry, beetroot, parsnip and raisin. The wine was plentiful and often potent.

Most homes had some special decorations. The front windows were polished until they shone like crystal. Across the middle of the windows there appeared sprigs of berried holly with oranges and rosy apples.

A mistletoe bough hung from every living room ceiling. Some were made of evergreens and others of frilled tissue paper of various colours, but all were decorated with fancy glass toys which were kept from one year to another.

At my own home, Christmas Eve supper was celebrated in the same way for many years. We gathered round a large table. The lamps were removed to a side table and replaced by two brass candlesticks containing coloured candles and decorated round the base with paper frills.

A big stew jar, full of frumenty, was brought from

the oven where it had been cooking for several hours. It was made with pearl wheat and milk and was served with sugar, cassia and more milk. This was followed by slices of Yule cake and Wensleydale cheese. The cheese was always a big four-to-five pound one, scraped on top, bottom and sides until it was perfectly clean. The sign of the cross was marked on top of it and a piece of holly with plenty of berries was pushed into the centre.

Jane Harrison (1971)

Tasting the Cake

Mary proceeded in solemn silence to remove a cloth from her Christmas cake as though she was ceremoniously unveiling a statue. Having turned it so that the aperture disclosed the black richness of the interior, she stood back with hands clasped and gazed in admiration.

The other ladies also gazed in silence. Betty slowly and reverently walked to the table for closer examination. The others did likewise in turn. They sighed sighs, and nodded nods, which, being interpreted, signified profound approval of the colour, wonder at the quantity of fruit, the baking, the size - everything about it so far as outward appearance went. Mr. Tiny hopped round the table as a lame and tame robin would do, uttering incoherent twitterings.

"It tastes - so others who know tell me - as good as it looks," announced Mary handing each lady a plate. This they placed on the handkerchiefs they had spread on their knees and, cutting a slab which she divided so that there was a piece for each person, Mary handed these to her guests in solemn state, watching each to read the innermost thoughts of their minds.

The silence continued as fitted the occasion till Mrs. Tiny, with head on the side and her left eye half-closed, began with a giggle: "I'll tell you where I think you've made a mistake, Mrs..........." She got not further. Mary bridled up and, as Betty described it later, "pounced at Mrs Tiny like a bull tiger."

"Some folks waits while they're asked for their 'pinions." There isn't no mistakes an' what's more this isn't a 'cashun for smirkin' and gigglin'. Tastin' a cake - leastways, such a cake as that - is summat ti be done careful, slow an' realisin' what you're a-doin of. You've had neither time nor experience nor as you, so to speak, called on, or qualified to criticise.

"I repeats there's no mistakes. That's a cake sich as I wadn't care if the Queen and all the Royal Family called to taste. If they spake the truth, they'd say they'd nivver tasted a better ..."

J Fairfax-Blakeborough (1951)

Christmas Morning

At 7am the first suggestion of dawn was turning the cloudless sky above Carlton Bank to a luminous steely blue. Poised there, as though resting one fragile point on the heather, was the last thin crescent of the December moon.

Close to it, very bright, was the morning Star, Venus. The dark and frozen fields were completely silent. No traffic moved for miles around. An owl hooted from the wood, and as the dawn-light strengthened a partridge twittered amongst the turnips, that was all; a quiet prelude to a day of frozen brilliance, of cold beauty outside and warm cheer within.

Bill Cowley (1989)

Up for t'Show

Short, dark days before Christmas are an oft-noticed feature of our Yorkshire weather, for the same period after the winter equinox is seldom as gloomy. The festival of Christmas could not be celebrated at a more apt time, as the preparations and friendly visits carry us over this dull period.

A well-timed event of the farming calendar is Smithfield Show, during the first few days of the month. At Smithfield one meets as many friends as at a Yorkshire market. The warmth and comfort is a welcome change from the mud and dank hedgerows of our native county.

Outside, the bright lights beckon and theatres and tubes are filled with rural accents from all parts of the land. Each year brings a crop of stories concerning Yorkshire farmers at large in "the Swinging City". My favourite harks back a year or two ago, when straw was a very good trade.

A farmer visited a night club and rather to his amazement a straw-skirted hostess perched herself on his knee and asked him to buy some drinks. Ignoring the request, our friend looked appreciatively at the straw skirt and said: "That's a bit o' reight stuff tha's gotten there, lass. If I had a few stacks o' that it'd be worth all of ten pund a ton".

Edward Hart (1966)

Plough Stots

On the first Monday after Twelfth Night there would be a great expedition to Goathland. This was Plough Monday. Mummy drove us some six or seven miles over the moor in her tiny Austin Seven, heaving with several more wriggling, excited youngsters than it was designed to carry.

With radiator steaming and chains slapping noisily

in the rough and frozen ruts of gritted snow, it could only just haul us up the long steep incline of Blue Bank. Then across the tops and down the 1-in-4, over the hump-backed pack bridge and into the normally sleepy and sheep-grazed village we slid and churned.

There on the green were the Plough Stots, dressed gawdily and jangling the bells of mummers and jesters; they entertained the crowd of farmers and everybody else from miles around. One old woman whom mummy said was really a man dressed up, played a squeaky fiddle while another handed round the cap which would, not doubt, later quench their thirst at the pub.

But it was the longsword dancers who really stole the show. How they danced and wove and flashed their silver swords, made patterns, reversed the movement, unravelled the design, flung up their weapons, caught them and wreathed another.

To us, these clever men in their silken suits with broad, coloured sashes and a red stripe down the leg were more exciting than a band of angels; they were real, they were strong and brave, dodging the flashing blades. Never once was one wounded - though that was quite a disappointment.

But would they never come to the point, the most thrilling part of all, when just once dancer held aloft all the intertwined swords in a triumphant six-pointed star? This is what we had specially come to see, but could never work how it was done try as we might with garden canes which always got broken in the experiment.

This was the final treat of the Christmas holidays, the details of which were recounted and compared for months to come ...

Joanne English (1993)

Coast and Wolds

The Gift

The day after the Second World War broke out, my younger brother and sister and I were evacuated to Staithes. Just before Christmas, all the evacuees were summoned to a house overlooking the harbour. I entered and was greeted by a sea of faces belonging to weather-beaten, keen-eyed fishermen dressed in thick, oily, black sweaters, blue trousers and huge orange boots.

I was overwhelmed when one by one we had to stand in the middle of the room and tell them what we would like for Christmas. After a bit of coaxing, I told them I would love some knitting wool and needles. Then I promptly forgot all about it.

When Christmas morning arrived, I woke up and was filled with joy as I felt the lumpy Christmas stocking heavy on my feet. I leaned over and pulled open the curtains to let in the early morning light. Then I slowly examined the contents of my stocking. I savoured the shiny, red apple; I put the large, round orange close to my nose and smelt its delicious tang;

I rattled the tube of Smarties and sampled a few.

Then I bit into the bright, gold penny to see if it was real and if it was as hard as the walnuts and almonds which nestled behind the one and only wrapped present which I'd saved until last. I couldn't even hazard a guess at what it could be and I put off the moment of discovery for as long as possible. I felt its shape, I smelt it and then, with anticipation rising within me, I opened it and gasped.

There in all its glory lay a beautiful little workbox. I lifted up the top and gazed in disbelief at the variety of miniature walls of every hue, from deep purple and pale pink. Some were striped in two colours, like candy.

The workbox also contained a few pairs of smooth, wooden knitting needles in different sizes. Delightedly I caressed the soft, delicate coloured wool and touched the satin-smooth needles. As I noted the assortment of sizes, I thought no one could ever receive such a wonderful gift.

Santa Claus appears in many shapes and many sizes, though usually he comes as a genial old gentleman with a luxuriant white beard and dressed in red. But in the first Christmas of the war for me, a skinny little homesick evacuee, Father Christmas was a group of weather-beaten, keen-eyed fishermen dressed in thick, black sweaters and with huge, orange boots on their feet.

Margo Coser (1992)

Turkey Lectern

It is said to have been a Yorkshireman who first introduced the turkey into England. When Sebastian Cabot made his voyage of discovery to America, William Strickland, of Boynton Hall, near Bridlington, sailed with him as lieutenant. He found wild turkeys in the New World and could not resist bringing several back to England.

Strickland chose a turkey in its pride as the emblem for his coat-of-arms. Not long ago, Mr F. Johnson designed a new lectern for Boynton Church as a memorial to the late Major Fred Strickland.

The customary eagle was displaced - by a turkey!

(1954).

White Christmases

From Filey Bay to Flamborough Head, the coast villages are our own again in winter. The holiday camps are closed and the bed-and-breakfast signs removed, but we don't exactly hibernate till crowds of people from the West Riding towns return to Reighton Gap and similar spots.

White Christmases are rare nowadays. It is unlikely that the road leading from "The Dotterel" to Speeton and Bempton will be blocked by snow when I set out to take services there. A little later, in the New Year, perhaps; but only twice in five years have I been unable to get through from Reighton to Speeton because of snow-filled ways. The council workmen will have erected the snow fences along the

Bridlington road, just in case.

It may well be that I shall be needed once again for the Midnight Communion of Christmas at Bempton, for at the time of writing no new vicar has been appointed. Bempton is a lovely little church, and always candlelit for this service. The church, which stands beside the village green and duckpond, serves also the twin village of Buckton. How did separate villages come to be so close together?

Bernard Croft (1973).

Flamborough's Day of Dance

Standing around in the streets of a coastal village at the end of December, with an icy wind whistling in from the North Sea, is not generally to be recommended. But if you can drag yourself away from your cosy fireside armchair...and get over to Flamborough on Boxing Day, you will be rewarded by the sight of

some fine dancing and the sounds of toe-tapping music. This is the only day in the year when it is possible to see the Flamborough longsword dance being performed in its native village by local men. I was also fortunate to be able to visit Mary Cross, who was then in her mid-80s and has since died. She taught the sword dance to many of the present generation of dancers when, as little boys, they attended the local infants' school.

When Mrs Cross had been a girl, and there were still plenty of fishermen living in the village, the young boys, including her brothers, learned the steps by watching fishermen perform the dance. Morris dancing encompasses a number of styles and traditions; the handkerchief-waving, stick-clashing style which originated in the Cotswolds, the clog dances of the north-west processional morris and Yorkshire's own longsword dance, similar to the short sword dances of the Tyneside miners.

The dancers meet at the Flameburgh Hotel about 11am and aim to dance outside the "Rose and Crown" by noon. They dance at various points in the village during the day, finishing in the late afternoon outside the "Dog and Duck" in the main square. During Mrs Cross's lifetime, they paid tribute to their old teacher by performing in front of her house, which delighted her.

There are no longer any fishermen in the side. The few old ones who still live in the village "look at us as if we are bloody daft," said one dancer. As with many of these old customs and traditions, one family has more than one member connected with it. In Flamborough it is the Treves family, with five.

One of Richard Treves' main jobs is to get the dancers out of the many pubs and hotels on their route and into the street to dance. "Too much drinking," said Richard, not unreasonably, "affects their ability to dance."

Julia Smith (1993).

Christmas Geese

On the Wolds farms, the second week of December will see a thinning out of poultry in the stockyards. Perhaps a couple of trios of geese and ducks will be left waddling around, the fore-runners of next year's stock.

The rest will be gathered in, probably shedding their snowy feathers into a large zinc bath, the pluckers sitting around with fingers blue, stiff and sore, their legs starved in the draught, and thinking (as they do in December of every year), that it will be the last time they raise stock for the Christmas market.

Friends who rear geese to supply regular private customers are so sentimental about their grand birds, after feeding and caring for them throughout the year, that the mother and daughter say they couldn't eat a bite of them; it would choke them. Father does not think this way, and when the geese are killed and dressed he takes them into town.

For a farming family's own dinner, a strange goose must be bought. I have been on a farm when a man has returned with the Christmas dinner, looking glum, dumped the goose, badly wrapped in a sheet of greasy paper, down on the kitchen table. "Here's your goose," he says, and probably adds: "It isn't as good as one of ours..."

Mother may say: "Wouldn't you think they would

wrap it up differently." And her daughter adds: " They might put the giblets separate."

Am I letting the cat out of the bag when I tell you I have met father in town seeking that brown paper to wrap about his own goose, the one he brought to market and planned to eat weeks ago? What the eye doesn't see, the heart will not grieve.

I once won a goose in a raffle. When it was delivered, it was such a poor thing that my husband said it must have been killed to save its life. On another occasion, I arranged with a man who owed me a debt to let me have a goose for Christmas dinner in payment. The goose came in a tea-chest. It was alive, so I sent it to my butcher to be killed and dressed. He reported: "If that goose had lived much longer, it would have been going around on crutches."

By which you will gather I am not very lucky where geese are concerned.

Florence Hopper (1968).

The Nervous Housewife

A tale which still goes the rounds of the Wolds concerns a wealthy old farmer who had a young and most attractive wife. She was a clever housewife, too, rearing lots of poultry which she helped to dress and which her husband took to the Christmas market.

With the proceeds from his sales tucked away in a leather bag, the farmer returned home, well satisfied with his day's work, when out from the side of the road a wayfarer stepped and begged a lift. The spirit of Christmas prevailing, the farmer took the stranger on board and found him such an agreeable companion he was invited to supper.

Together they stabled the horse and went into the house, the stranger being amazed at the attractiveness of the farmer's wife, at the wonderful supper she had prepared for him - and at the young woman's agitation and the way her eyes went again and again to the big cupboard by the fireside.

Supper over, the men began yarning. "There was a time," the stranger said, "when I could raise the devil!" The old farmer was more than impressed. "Mah wod," he said, "but ah'd like to see that." Talk continued, but the farmer's curiosity had been aroused.

"Ah'll tell tha what," said the stranger, "you set aboot raising the devil and ah'll gie yer half of the money that's in that bag." To show he really meant what he said, he threw the money-bag down on the table. The stranger demurred.

"Lookyer," the farmer said, "Ah'll raise me stakes. You raise the devil - and you can tak t'lot." That was what the stranger was waiting for. He lowered the lamp, borrowed the farmer's stick and with three heavy blows on the cupboard door he commanded: "Come out ye devil!"

The door flew open, upsetting the farmer from his chair, and a dark form sped across the kitchen and out of the door. "Did yer see him?" the stranger asked as he helped the farmer to his feet.

"Eh, ah did," the farmer said breathlessly, "and, by gum! He was the living spit of oor butcher."

Florence Hopper (1972).

THE
DECEMBER, 1960
1/-
DALESMAN

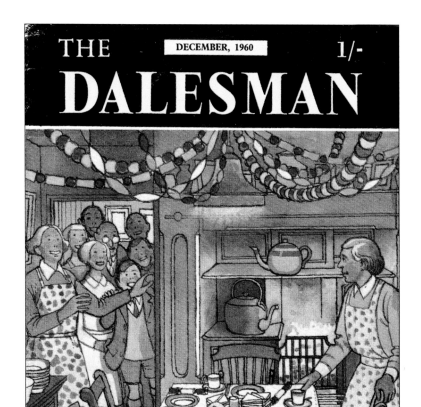

How the Dalesman marked Christmas 1960 through the eyes of Ionicus.

Skating Days

The frost had come for Christmas. The ponds in the fields and the puddles on the roads had a thin coating of ice. Everyone I met was muffled with clothing, complaining of the cold, and I recalled days gone by when the frost received a warmer welcome.

As children in an isolated village on the Yorkshire Wolds we watched the barometer, anxious lest the mercury rose too soon. Schoolchildren who were dawdling until the last stroke of the bell were usually the first with the exciting news. We were lucky to have two ponds, one at each end of the double row of houses, and as soon as these were well and truly covered, the saddler and his man laid aside their routine work, bringing out from dusty corners odd straps and buckles which had been forgotten during the summer.

Customers came in a continuous stream up the two high steps into the dimly-lit room which smelt deliciously of beeswax and leather. They brought with them every type of skate. There was the postman with heavy old iron "rat-traps", kept in place by an enormous heel-screw, and the vicar's son with his shining hollow-ground steel knife-edges.

The champion skater in our village was the innkeeper. Although well over 70, he would flash over the shining surface like a darting swallow, circling and spinning round us until we grew dizzy and staggered to the side-rail for support.

As the morning wore on, old Miss Milner pottered across from her tiny cottage with an apron full of hot potatoes baked in their "jackets", and we cupped them to our numb fingers, biting deeply into their floury hearts.

The frost never lasted long, so we made the most of the day. When it grew dark, we skated and slid and sang by the light of stable lanterns and car headlights. Those who lived nearby brought out steaming jugs of coffee and cocoa. In the tap-room of the "Black Swan", the inn-keeper, still in tweed knicker-bockers and polo-necked sweater, dispensed mulled ale to the elders.

Rosemary Rothwell (1950).

Christmas fayre worth queuing for at Otley by Clifford Robinson.

Above, inside
England's oldest
chemist shop in
Knaresborough
by Clifford
Robinson.

Right, brandy (the
vital ingredient)
being added to the
mincemeat at Colne
Valley Museum
by Clifford
Robinson.

5

South Yorkshire

Christmas Homecoming

I remember playing at Rotherham in my very early days on the stage. We were doing a good old melodrama, "Cripple Creek", and as the title denotes it was a western mining drama. The three acts all take place in a gold mine, and the villains are trying to steal the mine from the goodies.

A cage suspended from the "flies" was the only means of reaching the mine workings. It was Christmas Eve and, as we did not play on Christmas Day, I decided that after the show I would go and spend that day with my people at Handsworth, Birmingham.

The play was well on its way when the first accident happened. The cage containing the villain and his fellow baddies collapsed and fell on to the stage 20 feet below. The only casualty, much to the delight of the audience, was number one baddie who had given his nose a painful jab on the edge of the scenery. He finished the act with blood streaming from his nose and everyone in the audience marvelled at how realistic it all was, bloody nose included.

In a second accident, the hero, or "head goodie", put out a powder trail set to blow us all to pieces and forgot the stage directions. He tried to extinguish it with his bare hands and sustained some bad burns. The show must go on, but a third incident occurred - to me.

I was playing a West African all blacked up and curly-wigged. Unfortunately, the wig had failed to arrive, so my hair was given a "permanent" with curling tongs. The show over, I dashed for my train, arriving in Birmingham in the early hours of Christmas Day. To my astonishment, I was refused admission at the first attempt to my " ancestral" home and the door was slammed in my face.

After several attempts, I at last gained admission, only to discover that in my rush for the train I had completely forgotten to remove my black make-up. That, with my tightly curled hair, was sufficient reason for my being locked out.

Victor Tandy (1969)

Seasonal Ditties

The festive season prompts me to write about an old South Yorkshire mining area custom of "wishing" at Christmas and on New Year's Eve. "Wishing" on Christmas Eve seems to have faded out. It was floundering in the area in the middle 1940s and no doubt faded away in the affluent 1950s. The tradition of "wishing" at the New Year is still carried on in the local villages of Thorpe Hesley and Scholes.

I remember the following Christmas ditties, handed

down from my grandfather to his father and then on to me, and recited with vigour by lads in the village. On Christmas Eve, the following was the favourite rhyme:

Wish you Merry Christmas
And a Happy New Year.
I'm Teetotal and I want no beer.
A bit of spice-cake and a small bit o' cheese,
A glass of cold water and a penny if you please.
If you haven't got a penny, a ha'penny will do.
If you haven't got a ha'penny, God Bless You.

Here's another very old wishing rhyme:

Wish you Merry Christmas and a Happy New Year,
Pocket full o' money and a cellar full o' beer.
A great fat pig to kill next year,
An apple and a pear, a plum and a cherry,
A bit o' spiced cake to make a man merry.

Phil Parkin (1972).

West Yorkshire

Bradford Sunbeams

Pantomime-time brings memories of a great theatrical tradition. The Sunbeam tradition began in 1913 when Francis Laidler, the impressario who built Bradford's Alhambra Theatre, was rehearsing his pantomimes for the coming season.

His young dancers had previously been called "The Pantomime Girls" or the "Princes' Children". Mr

41

Laidler was arranging touring pantomimes to other theatres so it seemed a good idea to have a single name for all his dancing troupes and the one name was officially adopted.

Theatrical tradition has it that suggestions were placed in a hat. The smallest girl dancer is supposed to have drawn out a slip of paper which said "Sunbeams" but she might just as easily have chosen "Starlets" or "Tinies" or "Twinkles".

What was it like to be chosen as a Sunbeam? Mary Cunningham, of Bradford, had attended an audition at the old Prince's Theatre in Bradford and remembered the six-deep queue winding round and round the building. Lots of eager little girls with their equally anxious mums were waiting for the stage doors to open at 10am. Some of them had been there since 7.30am!

The girls had to walk past a chalk mark on a wall which showed the maximum height for a Sunbeam. They would then be shown a short dance sequence and asked to dance it themselves. They had to walk from wing to wing, sing a short piece and smile at Mr. Laidler. He was always wanting the girls to look up, smile and "put on a happy face".

The girls who were chosen initially had to wait around for a further, more stringent audition. Then if they were successful they could call themselves Sunbeams! "If you had been chosen," said Mary, "you wanted all the world to know. You felt like a star, you were a star! My mother was even more pleased than I was, if you can imagine that. She had my hair cut straight away so then everyone knew I was a Sunbeam. The haircut was special, you see, a fringe with a short bob and we had to have it cut fortnightly."

All Sunbeams have special and warm memories of

the way they were looked after. Each girl was the responsibility of a matron, known forever to her young charges as "Aunty".

Kevin Berry (1990)

Annie's Christmas

It had been traditional for my dad's cousin Annie and her widowed mother to spend Christmas with my grandparents at their village shop. I loved to hear her recollections of those Christmases at the turn of the century and just after. Annie was entrusted with parcelling up the little presents they had managed to scrape together, while waiting for the sound of her mother's key in the lock. Then it really was Christmas Eve, and time to set out for "Uncle John's" at the other side of the town.

Annie knew that Santa had to budget, as her mother did, so she didn't hope for anything special. Perhaps it might run to an orange, a packet of nuts and raisins and a bright new penny. After all, she had been taught that it was the atmosphere that counted, the carol singing, going to church and all that. Besides, she and her mother would have a warm bed for the night and lovely "proper" meals the next day. What more could anyone expect?

By half past nine on Christmas Eve, the three children had had their "pobs" - a concoction of warm milk with bread dropped in. They had draped three black woollen stockings from the rail in front of the Yorkshire range. As she snuggled down beneath the blankets, Annie would hear the boys whispering to each other in their bedroom across the landing. She heard the "plop" of the gas jet as they turned off the light.

After saying her prayers, Annie made sure there was a good half of the bed spare for when her mother came up. Then it seemed no time at all before, from a deep and dreamless sleep - when not even Christmas morning mattered any more - she felt herself being nudged gently. "Wake up, sleepy-head - listen, the band's playing." Faintly at first, then louder, came the sounds of the village brass band playing "Christian's Awake", pausing at various landmarks on their way, the shop being one of them.

The grown-ups were busy all morning about the house, while Annie, Alfred and Joe played on the rug before the kitchen fire. One year Annie was thrilled to find a Diabalo set in her stocking. Another Christmas morning there was a wonderful monkey which did acrobatics, over and over, on a stick.

The boys and Annie later went to chapel with Uncle John while the ladies prepared the vegetables, plum pudding and pork with stuffing. A crackling bright coal fire was soon glowing in the upstairs front room as well as in the living-kitchen, in readiness for "company" at dinnertime.

After morning service, Annie was overjoyed to be asked to "set the table" with the best cutlery. Grandad had a machine on which, on special occasions, knives could be cleaned. Glasses were placed alongside, with a big jug of water in the centre of the table. Being staunch Methodists, no one expected, or even wanted, wine with the dinner.

Going up for noon, Aunt Polly and Uncle William arrived with little gifts for everybody, the gifts wrapped in brown paper, with sprigs of bright red holly tied with string. After much jollity and kissing beneath the mistletoe, outdoor clothes were ceremoniously laid on the eiderdown in the big bedroom.

Hair was rearranged, "buns" fixed with hair grips, snippets of news not meant for gentlemen's ears exchanged before glasses of elderberry wine which Grandad had made. This was sipped upstairs in the front room, from diminutive containers, while Annie, Alfred and Joe were allowed to have ginger beer. The children waited with bated breath while Aunt Polly handed out the presents.

After Christmas dinner, the afternoon was enlivened when everyone sang carols round the piano. Then it was time for high tea. What a spread! Cold pork, stuffing, cranberry sauce, brown and white bread, trifles lost beneath lashings of fresh cream and decorated with "hundreds of thousands". A huge round Christmas cake and Stilton cheese were "washed down", as Uncle William used to remark, with lots of good strong tea. It created another load of washing up.

The chenille cloth was restored to the table and the aspidistra placed exactly in the centre, with the family Bible. Then there was just time for a few games before another Christmas Day at the village shop passed into the realms of history.

Hazel Wheeler (1986)

Under the Barber's Pole

"Ah see tha's been doin' a bit o' decoratin' for Kesmus, Barber," said Farmer Platt. "A bit o' holly an' mistletoe sets a place off Ah must say."

"It's th'wife's doin'," said the Barber. "Hoo's fond o'

that soart o' thing."

"Ah notice hoo's put th'mistletoe o'er my seat," said Owd Thatcher.

"It'll cost thee a new pair o' gloves," said Jim Gregson. "That is if hoo kisses thee."

"Tha said if," said the barber's wife. "It'll tak more nor a new pair o' gloves to make me kiss that lot."

"Nah then love," said Thatcher. "Tha needn't be shy about it. What about th'mince pies?"

"Ah've made yo' one apiece," said Sally.

"That's the idea," said Jim Gregson. "Kesmus is the time for a bit o' gutsin'."

"An' suppin'," said Owd Thatcher. "Dunnot leave that out."

"Tha never forgets that part," said Sally. "Thar't a reight owd swill tub."

"It's nobbut an excuse for gormandisin," said Young Winterburn. "Some on yo' fair makes a god o' yo're bellies."

"Let thisel' goo a bit, Winterburn." said Thatcher. "Get summat down thi chimbley while it's free."

"Ah like to be hospitable at this time," said Farmer Platt. "Anybody as comes to our house at Kesmus is welcome to a slice o' turkey an' a drop o' what's gooin'."

"What time do yo' get up, Farmer?" said Thatcher. "Ah'll be theer."

"Ah call it makin' a pagan festival on it," said Young Winterburn. "Yo' should be down on yo're knees instead o' sittin' up to th'table all th'time."

"Ah hope to finish on me back," said Thatcher.

"Tha would," said Sally. "Tha allus does. Tha should ha' been a barrel."

"What a pretty thought," said Thatcher.

T. Thompson (1950).

Ilkley church at Christmas by Colin Raw.

Winter in Golden Acre Park by Clifford Robinson.

The Mansion House, St Helens Square, York by Deryck Hallam.

The Choir singing in the Main Square at Grassington,
by Jacqui Cordingley.

Off to t'Messiah

One of the strangest performances of Messiah I attended was given in a "tin tabernacle" - a chapel formed of corrugated iron - at Skipton. Having accommodated the principals, an "augmented choir" and a dozen instrumentalists, the organisers found there was not much space for the congregation.

Everyone hoped for a fine day. In rainy weather, the roof leaked and drops of water had to be intercepted by several well-placed buckets. At service time, someone put a cloth in each bucket to deaden the sound!

Handel's famous oratorio was first performed in Dublin at Easter, but when the West Riding took the piece to its heart, it became a pre-Christmas attraction. The big town chapels could invite principals of national renown and muster upwards of 100 fine voices. Small chapels, rather less musical in their presentation of Messiah, had none the less their large

band of supporters, each of them familiar with the oratorio and ready to discuss fine points of interpretation at the interval.

On the whole, Yorkshire Messiah-goers liked the presentation clear and straight-forward. Some principals were apt to add "fancy bits". No one thought of clapping, of course, but you could sense the chilliness of the reception if a principal lacked zest, or the organist fluffed some notes, or someone in the choir over-ran into one of the Great Pauses in a chorus.

Chapel organs were tuned to the exacting Messiah standards. Choirs met once or twice for rehearsals of an oratorio known to all. There were choristers who held an open score only because it was expected of them; they did not actually look at it!

Several hundred voices rendered a Christmas hymn to begin the day's events. Some families stayed at the chapel between performances for a light meal. By the time the Amen Chorus was being lustily rendered, everyone was emotionally drained.

In the old days, there was such rivalry between chapels of various denominations that at the end of the evening performance, at each place, an expectant hush descended. A steward mounted the steps to the pulpit, holding a piece of paper and announcing how much money had been raised by the collections.

"Aye," he might add, "and that's £20 more than t'Wesleyans and £22 more than Bethel." You couldn't do better than that.

W. R. Mitchell (1985)

Christmas in Skipton by Colin Raw.

Picturesque, but life becomes tough for Littondale farmers, even at Christmas by Colin Raw.

Preparing for Christmas in this shop in Haworth by Clifford Robinson.

Christmas at Adel

Fifty years ago I was a schoolmaster at Adel. When Christmas came round, we spent weeks beforehand practising traditional carols. With boys up to 17 and 18 years of age, we could get four parts.

Choral singing was a feature of the school not only at Christmas but at other times, when concerts were given and such good pieces as The Madrigal from "The Mikado", "Three Fishers" and "Oh Peaceful Night" were well rendered.

The chairman of the management committee always welcomed the choir and the carol singers, who at midnight had to sing at the four corners of the house and also in the hall. Afterwards we were provided with hot coffee and Christmas "eats".

The schoolmasters put something - 80% proof - into their coffee to keep the cold out. In those days, the best whiskey could be obtained for 4s.6d a bottle, beer was 2s a gallon, 50 cigarettes could be bought for 1s.2d and a quarter of a pound of popular dark flake tobacco cost 1s.8d.

J. W. Maybury (1966)

Bairn's Kesmass

They come to tell me, Kesmass morn,
As how at Jesus Christ wor born.
They nivver knawed in t'starleet dim
Ah'd seed thruff t'mistal door a glim,
An heeard a chap to t'woman say:
"Ay why, there's nowt so warm as hay!"
An then Ah heeard a babby cry,

An angils singin' up in t'sky -
No call to tell me, Kesmass morn,
As how at t'babby Christ wor born.

Gwen Wade (1967).

Hebden Bridge in winter by Jacqui Cordingley.

7

The Pennine Dales

Conservation

Christmas in the Dales!
The children all agog
Round blazing hearth of festive flames
And ancient yuletide log:
Out there, across the yard,
The Christ-child's lowly stable,
And round our fire a cosy peace,
And on our plenteous table
Christmas cake, custom-baked,
Married to Wensleydale cheese...

Such simple things are all we need
To set the heart at ease -

But, country folk, beware!
There's a vandal who shows no pity:
If telly rules Christmas you might as well be
Deep in some grim inner city!

Arnold Kellett

Chapel with a Dome

On the last day of the Christmas term at Giggleswick School, the chapel on the hill is packed with pupils and parents for the annual carol service, which is a notable musical occasion as well as reminding all who attend of the true spirit of the season. The acoustics in this Victorian fantasy - this Gothic church with an Oriental dome - are at their best if every seat is occupied.

Two Christmases ago, when the BBC filmed a Russell Harty party from his home locally, we saw him visit the chapel in a sunset glow that added to the drama of the place. The television personality recalled that 30 years before, he arrived as a young schoolmaster to sit in "this incongruously grand chapel" and he was still thrilled by "the satisfying rituals of the annual carol service".

More than a few in the congregation this year will recall the brief chapel sequence - the faces of the choristers in the candle glow, the sense of mystery imparted by the ponderous dome and a glimpse of Russell Harty making his way from the chapel in the gloaming. He died in 1987 aged 53.

Domes are not common in England. The nearest to Giggleswick is that of the Ashton Memorial at Lancaster. The chapel, a gift to his old school from Walter Morrison, the Craven millionaire, commemorates the diamond jubilee of Queen Victoria. A picture of the new chapel, having been exhibited at the Royal Academy, was then sent to Balmoral for inspection by the Queen, who expressed her admiration of the design.

The copper dome which developed a greenish hue can easily be seen because the chapel is perched on a gritstone knoll, high above the School it serves. One who has known it for many years described the inside as "magnificent" and the outside as being "rather squat". People had told him that it was designed to fit the landscape. "I don't think it does, but for all that I am very fond of the place."

The foundation stone was laid on October 7, 1897, by the Duke of Devonshire. There followed four years of uninterrupted building work. The walls of the chapel were made from millstone grit quarried on the spot. Red sandstone was brought from Lazonby, in the Eden Valley. Limestone blocks came from Mr. Delaney's quarry at Horton-in-Ribblesdale. The window traceries were hewn from an especially hard and durable Lees Moor sandstone.

The dome which gives distinction to this hilltop chapel was constructed of interlocking blocks of terracotta, the outside being of timber covered with copper and the lining of the dome carried out with glass mosaic, devised by the architect. It was not worked from the back and afterwards reversed - the usual procedure - but fixed bit by bit on the vault and worked from the face. Each piece of glass is about the size of a sugar lump.

L. P. Dutton, who had a long and distinguished association with Giggleswick as second master, told me of old-time carol services at the chapel. In the early part of the 1939-45 war, when the black out was introduced and no naked light was to be shown from buildings at night, the headmaster, Mr. Partridge, insisted the end-of-term service should be held here, so a test was arranged.

The two men visited the chapel after dark and left two lighted candles on the floor in the chancel. The men then went outdoors to see the effect. The chapel looked like a beacon. The answer was to hold the service in the dark, apart from a small torch which the headmaster would use when reading passages of scripture.

Meanwhile, Charlie Cresswell would stand outside and report immediately if he heard approaching aircraft. Once or twice, Mr Dutton conducted the service. "When you went up to the altar for the final prayers, it was the loneliest place on earth because you could not see anyone else."

W. R. Mitchell (1988)

Snow After Christmas

It was at Grassington, a week after Christmas, that we were snowed up. We had walked to Drebley the afternoon before, but although it was bitterly cold and flecks of powdery snow blew in our faces when we returned, we were not prepared for the scene to which

we wakened the next morning.

Familiar landmarks in the Market Square were obliterated, and a terrific blizzard swept across it, piling the snow into drifts. Telegraph wires were down and others leaned at all angles. One bus reached the bridge but could not mount the hill. It was the last bus which made the attempt that day.

Swiftly and persistently the snow cut us off from the rest of the world. Hundreds of sheep were overblown in that storm and it was more than a week before the electric light or a proper telephone service were restored, but I have never seen anything to surpass for pure beauty of Grass Wood that evening after the blizzard was spent.

Snow has little terror for dales children. They tramp unconcernedly to school in it, and a slight fall will bring them out to make for the nearest hill with their sledges.

But it is not always snowing. There are clear, frosty days when the hills are whitened with a more subtle brush, but so firmly that strong sunshine cannot move it. On such days, the sinking sun gives an alpine glow to the hilltops, a delicate rosiness which makes you catch your breath at the wonder of it.

Ella Pontefract (1939).

A Dales Farmer's Diary

1946. Christmas Day. The greetings cards are set out all round the room, and all have the usual snow and farmers driving the sheep through the village scene. Some of the houses are lit up, according to the cards, as if we would be out driving sheep on

Christmas Night.

1947. The lads, God bless them, gave me a present of a few cigars...of all smokes, I enjoy a cigar the best. It was a quiet Christmas, no music from any carollers, but we had plenty to eat, and in these times that is something. Had to be content with a duck for our lot, and there was only enough plum pudding for one meal, and that without any rum in the sauce. What a tragedy!

1948. What is there about Christmas which makes us all so affable? It is essentially a time for children, and I wonder if seeing them so happy makes us happy also. Had a novel Christmas present. Our old bitch presented us with five puppies.

1950. A delightful day. Recalled there was not a big post yesterday. The postman would not come in for his customary drink. He whispered to me that he had had several stiff glasses "in view of the cold". He was afraid he would not be able to get round if he had any more.

Drake Ghyll (Norman Thornber).

The Feizor Ball

(Feizor is a secluded hamlet near Austwick).

An event associated with the Yuletide festivities of an almost forgotten past was the annual "Feizor Ball". On the evening it was held, all roads led to Feizor, and guests were arriving by gig, trap and cart.

The festivities were held in the "big house" at the higher end of the hamlet. A large room was decorated and specially illuminated with lamps and candles.

Adjoining this room was the spacious kitchen, where at one end stood a washing or set-boiler.

Music was provided by an old fiddler, a capable player, but a bit "rheumaticky" in his lower limbs. While playing for the dancing, the old man sat on the boiler with his feet tucked inside the bowl, giving the appearance of having lost both legs below the knee.

This unique musician's gallery was warmed up occasionally by burning wisps of straw in the boiler fireplace; ideal conditions, one would imagine, for interpreting "hot jazz." But this was long before modern music found a place in any dance programme.

The lively gatherings that once brought fame to Feizor are gone for ever.

Frederic Riley (1946).

Absent Friend

Ee Luv! we cannot clasp thi hand
Nor share wi' thee us caake;
T'Yule Loaf an' t'furmenty
As noan like Mum can maake.
But we can wish thee ivvery good
'At Kessimas can bring,
An' in t'year 'at follows on
T'best of ivvery thing.

E. K. S. (1949)

Christmas Yarns

Round a Christmas fire I first heard of the young angler who had been sitting by the side of the pool from early morning until well into the afternoon hoping for a tell-tale dip of his float. Along the pathway came a stranger who asked the lad if he had caught anything.

"Aye," was the reply, "I have that!"

"What?" asked the other.

"Patience," was the reply.

Another story at a Christmas gathering was of Old Joe who had the reputation of being able to catch fish when all other anglers failed. Among the many who admired and envied him was the local doctor. Came the day when the old angler was sinking fast.

"Joe, my old friend," said the doctor. "For many years, I've envied the ease with which you catch fish. I'll give you five pounds if you tell me the secret of your success."

The veteran nodded his head. "Gie t'fiver to t'missus," he said. When the note was handed over, the doctor bent low to hear what advice the old man had to offer. "Doctor," whispered Joe, "thou mun larn to strike whenivver thou gets a bite."

Broughton Point (T. K. Wilson), 1951

Christmas at Leyburn

(Fred Lawson, the Wensleydale artist, sent us a monthly letter, featuring a sketch and notes. Fred wrote pretty much as he spoke).

It seems strange that we have had Christmas. It was such a nice back-end that Christmas seemed to come all of a sudden. We spent it at Leyburn. It was grand for us to be all together.

December 24th was so mild and foggy, you could hardly see the market from the causeway by the shops. They had a nice Christmas tree, and with the stalls all round it, it looked very seasonable.

I like Christmas trees, public ones with their coloured lights, or private ones with their coloured balls, tinsel and fairies, and if there is a crib by the side it is perfect!

Going up the market place on Christmas Day I began to wonder why it was deserted - not one person and only two parked cars. I looked to see what time it was; it was a quarter to one; the great feast was on.

I went and sat on a seat on the Shawl. A fine sunny morning, the river below like silver, and far away in a warm haze, the hills of Coverdale. On my way back I met a private bus, full of people coming into Leyburn, just like summer.

I have still a long list of cards to send off, and now it looks a bit hopeless. I trust that I shall be forgiven. Among all the good wishes I received was a bill, just as plain statement - not even a verse.

Fred Lawson (1958)

Root and Branch

I climbed a thickly wooded rise
Along a wintry Pennine Way
When through the trees, to my surprise,
Came voices. Then I heard one say:
"There's berries here. This lot'll do.
Hold back that branch, I'll hack it through."

Later I searched the spot and found
Mangled roots and rough-splintered wood.
Torn branches lay on trampled ground
Where a bright holly bush had stood.
Beauty laid waste - to deck a hall
Or bunch for sale on market stall?

A.T.

Busking at Clapham

All the local brass bands played Christmas music around the villages at the festive season. Giggleswick band would travel on the 7.10am train to Clapham on Christmas Day and call at the "Flying Horseshoe" before walking up to the village.

After playing at Mr. Farrer's, we were provided with

CLAPHAM

E·GOWER

a good breakfast. The rest of the day we played at all the farms, including Austwick and Lawkland, walking many times up to the knees in snow, till we arrived at Giggleswick.

By this time we had imbibed our fair share of the "cup that cheers" and could not hold up the instruments, let alone play, so we burst into song instead!

I was the youngest member of the band and played the bass trombone. I well remember one Christmas when the hot punch bowl was passed round at the "Flying Horseshoe". Having had a good breakfast before starting out, we could not drink it all. One of the men said: "Let's tak it wi' us, Johnny! Thee put it in th' trombone and we'll hev a sup on t'rooad, but be careful ta 'od it reight side up - and don't play."

I did as I was told and the good old punch was disposed of by the men o' brass before we entered the village of Clapham.

John Walmsley Heelis (1955)

The Teesdale Illusion

For several years now, a group of slightly eccentric friends have gone to Middleton-in-Teesdale to walk some life into a system made sluggish by a surfeit of Christmas fare. We chose this walk because, like an old-fashioned round Christmas pudding - now sadly seldom if ever seen - it contained all the ingredients we deemed to be essential for a good Christmas walk.

At 12 miles, the length was right and the scenery was to our liking. The lovely Tees was never far away, and there was a beguiling simplicity about the route. A friendly hostelry stood at the half way point, and the way back was simply the reverse of the way there, which allowed us to switch to "automatic pilot" and concentrate on rendering favourite seasonal melodies as we walked along.

For the first few years, we experienced every sort of weather except that without which the walk could never be called truly seasonal. We craved for snow and it never came. Then, at last, we got our wish. It snowed and snowed and better snowed. Secondary roads were filled hedge-top high and strong winds flung smooth ridges of snow across the highway. For a while, the combined effects of wind and snow brought northern England to a standstill.

When we set off for Middleton that late December morning we had doubts about getting there; but, despite a few encounters with drifts, we made it and found the car park empty. The place had taken a pasting. Heavy snowfalls carried on fierce winds had become smothering snow dunes through which narrow passageways had been cut leading from dwellings and shops to the middle of the main street, where a path wide enough for cars to pass along in single file had been cleared.

The Tees, with its icy wind, flowed darkly through a sparkling winter wonderland, a fantasy etched in black and white that had all the makings of a Victorian Christmas card scene. This, then, was the splendid setting for our walk. No wonder our spirits soared.

If anything, our journey became more enchanting the further we progressed. Aided by pale sunshine, the white mantle sparkled like crushed diamonds. Tracks of rabbit, hare and fox, together with those of various birds, whetted our interest and gave us food for thought. At times we ploughed through deep drifts and at others we made faster progress across exposed areas swept clean of all but a thin cover of snow through which bleached stems of vegetation protruded.

We rejoined the Tees and continued upstream alongside it, sharing this part of our journey with pied wagtails and dippers. With the ground frozen hard, it was difficult to imagine the richness of flora that would appear come spring.

At the inn near High Force we could have had turkey or goose or chicken but we had taken a surfeit of such fare lately and craved something different. I settled for hotpot, with something strong to wash it down, for the time had come to indulge in a little wassailing. The name comes from two Anglo-Saxon words, was hael, meaning "Be thou hale", from which we have "Good health!" This salutation is offered with a drink, usually presented with a bowl which is passed from hand to hand as everyone drinks in fellowship.

The strangest part of the return was that the snow took on a rosy tincture. In fact, the whole wide world had about it a suffusion of rosiness. Wassailing has that effect on people.

Charlie Emett (1985)

8

Aspects of Christmas

Snowtime at Cosh

Among the isolated farms where snow might lie for months on end was Cosh, two and a-half miles beyond Foxup, which itself is remote, being tucked away at the head of Littondale. Early this century, the Brown family of Cosh thought nothing of walking five miles to Horton to catch a train or driving some of their Swaledale ewes for ten miles to market at Hawes. For Christmas, they had their own company.

One December, the snow lay at Cosh for so long there was a danger that the sheep might starve. So William Brown gathered them, mounted his pony and drove the sheep across the glistening landscape looking for green fields where farmers might provide grazing for a penny or two per sheep. There were 450 ewes and a few tups.

The first night was spent with friends at Neils Ing, "back o' Penyghent". The flock was then moved on towards the Ribble Valley, where, at farms around Wigglesworth, Mr Brown found quarters for his sheep

65

for a whole month. The hospitable farmers referred to the stock from Cosh as "them snowbound sheep".

In 1917, another bad winter, one of the sheep at Cosh spent three weeks under snow - and lived to bleat the tale. That ewe was 14 years old when she died accidentally, having wandered into a dipping tub when there was no one about to rescue her.

Winter was a gloomy time at Cosh. Robert Brown, son of William, recalls milking the house cow at Cosh when light was provided by a candle stuck on a "through end" in the shippon. He sat on a three-legged stool.

The Browns of Cosh and families living at other remote farms laid in special stores for winter use. Richard Brown remembers a ten stone bag of white flour. The pig-killer, John Cowan of Halton Gill, had to have a little drop of whisky "or t'pig wouldn't cure properly"! Several days after the animal was killed, John and several farmers returned to cut it up - and to play cards for the rest of the long winter night.

W R Mitchell (1984)

"Old-fashioned" Christmas

Those who lament the passing of the "old-fash-ioned" Christmas, with its customs and rituals and memories, may take heart. One at least of the old accompaniments of Christmas may be on its way back.

Was it not a north-countryman who a century or more ago set down the famous lines:

First it rain, and then it blew,
Then it friz and next it snew.
And rained again, and with it thew
And friz again. Oh misery!

A "white Christmas" of this sort has been a rarity of recent years, but we are now told that a long cold spell may be upon us in which we shall have winters similar to those long ago, when folk skated on our Yorkshire rivers, with hot chestnut stalls to cater for them; when the fields always wore white robes for Christmas, and when all the water butts froze.

A typical entry of over a century ago is this from John Mayhall's Annals of Yorkshire: "A very strong frost commenced and prevailed for about six weeks. The river Aire was frozen over and afforded good skating above Leeds. Inland navigation was entirely suspended..."

One reason for the "old-fashioned" Christmas, it has been suggested, is that prior to 1752, when eleven days were cut out of the calendar, Christmas Day fell on what is now January 5, a time when snow and frost are far more probable. So a white Christmas was then more seasonable.

H J S (1970)

Mr Parker's Favourite Tune

Every Christmas morning, before the 1939-45 war, Haworth Brass Band arrived in the back yard of the village's Merrall's Mill and played the hymn tune "Deep Harmony". As they played, Abraham - the tenant of the Mill House, who had started work as a half-timer and was now company secretary - sat in his rocking chair and "tears rolled down his face".

The story was told to me by his son, John Scarborough, a great-nephew of Handel Parker, the composer of "Deep Harmony" and many another good hymn tune. To several generations of West Riding folk, this tune, set to Isaac Watts's hymn "Sweet is the Work", was very special, being used widely by choirs and brass bands.

The Black Dyke Mills Band popularised it by playing the tune after every concert. At its most celebrated

Joseph Appleyard

period, "Deep Harmony" was recorded on gramophone records and played fairly often, by special request, on "t'wireless". For me, it evokes images of the old West Riding, with its mills, chapels and countless amateur music-makers.

Handel Parker was born at Oxenhope, in a family with strong Haworth connections. Nearly all the Parkers were "musical". Handel's father, Abraham, whose daily work was that of coachman to the mill-owner, William Greenwood, knew the Bronte family well. Abraham was an exponent of the clarinet and violin.

Handel's mother, Martha, had been christened at Haworth in 1825 by the Rev Patrick Bronte. Her fine voice did not desert her to her dying day, at the age of 85. She sang for the doctor attending her in her last illness and is reported to have "hit the top notes". It is believed that Patrick Bronte solemnised the marriage of her grandparents and that Charlotte Bronte, when she was a young girl, occasionally called at the Parker home and played on Abraham's harmonium.

Abraham and Martha named their children after individuals who had become famous in the musical world - after Handel (the first-born), Miriam, Jubal, Haydn, Frederick and Sarah (Frederick was to have been christened Mozart but his mother changed the name when a neighbour said it sounded like "Noah's Ark."

Handel, a precocious child, who soon developed a passion for music, started work in t'mill, Greenwood's mill, where he was taught wool-sorting. Handel is said to have sorted the first bale of mohair which came into England. He left the mill at the age of 20 and embarked on a full-time musical career.

"Deep Harmony" was composed in 1867, nearly 40 years before it was first published. When it was recorded as a gramophone record by Besses o' th'Barn Band, the conductor, Alec Owen, referred to the hymn tune's "stately sonorousness in majesty and symmetry."

Handel himself made scarcely anything out of his hymn-writing. He died a relatively poor man. The funeral service was in Shipley Parish Church. In accordance with Handel's wish, a combined choir sang two hymns to music he had composed. One was a setting to "Abide with Me". The other was, of course, "Sweet is the Work" to the tune - "Deep Harmony".

W R Mitchell (1991)

Richmond's "Poor aud 'Oss"

The long dark nights of winter can be very frightening to small children whose imagination runs riot. The horse which might be encountered in lonely lanes around Richmond at Christmas-time is no figment of a fevered imagination. There are attendant huntsmen and hornblower. A very substantial six-foot man is hidden under the horse's head.

The "poor aud 'oss" is the leading character in a mummer's play which has been performed, more or less continuously each Christmas for generations. Bill Ward, who takes the part of one of the huntsmen, is a member of a family which has been deeply involved with it.

They have kept the play alive in the family even when it was impossible to perform it outside because they could not muster a team. Fortunately, "Oss" can be seen once again in the town, a team having been mustered. Alongside Billy are two sets of father and son, two exiles who travel from Darlington and an RAF station in Scotland and 13-year-old Jonathan, the son of Billy's cousin.

In 1989, as an observer, I joined the group on a dry, mild night in late December. Finishing touches were added to costumes, top hats were decorated with holly and mistletoe and the Christmas roses and poinsettias adorning "t'aud 'oss" were given a final check, before we set off through the dark streets.

The first stop was at a private house where a Christmas party was in full swing. The hornblower, an ex-trumpeter blowing a horn which once belonged to the Quorn Hunt, announced the arrival of the players. As the door was opened, the musician struck up the opening notes of the song which accompanies the play.

The story tells the story of a horse who is turned into open fields with short grass to nibble. He remembers when, in his prime, he had the best corn and hay and was ridden by his master in the hunting field. He is so weary he would rather die than live - and proceeds to do so. As this is a mumming play, he rises up again, death and revival being an integral part of any such performance.

The remaining stops that night were at pubs, some close by and others further afield at Brompton-on-Swale, Skeeby and Gilling.

Julia Smith (1991)

The Devil's Knell

On Christmas Eve at Dewsbury
They toll the Devil's Knell
To celebrate Old Nick's defeat
And keep him down in hell.

A peal for every year since Christ
They cheerfully discharge:
Oh, pull those bell-ropes harder, lads!
The Devil's still at large.

Arnold Kellett (1988)

The Hawes Junction Disaster

During the early part of this century, the working

hours of many railwaymen were long and demanding. The various railway companies gave little thought to factors such as stress and overwork...

In the early hours of Christmas Eve, 1910, signal-man Alfred Sutton was on duty in Hawes Junction signal-box, not many miles from the summit of the Settle-Carlisle. An early morning storm was wreaking havoc with the signal-lamps and the rain, driven into a wild curtain by the wind, made visibility a problem.

Sutton had little time to dwell on the outside elements. The past few hours had witnessed an almost relentless stream of traffic on his section of the line, and his concentration had been put to the test. A telegraph bell burst into life. Sutton turned to deal with an express approaching from the south.

Beyond the signal-box, movements in and around the station yard began to quicken in pace as two coupled tender engines from Carlisle took up position ready to move on to the turntable. Meanwhile, the down-express which Sutton had been anticipating charged through the station in a flurry of light.

HAWES JUNCTION DISASTER. XMAS EVE 1910

The two Carlisle engines left the turntable and moved slowly to take up position near the platform. There they awaited the signal which would send them on their journey home. Two goods trains heading south came and went. Up in the signal box, Sutton noted their progress in his register before preparing himself a mug of tea. The next train due was the midnight sleeping-car express from St Pancras to Glasgow.

The phone rang. Sutton's opposite number in Dent box spoke gruffly down the line: "She's running late but making up time." Sutton registered the call and crossed over to his signal-frame, making the line clear for the express and altering his signals accordingly. He was blissfully unaware that he was paving the way for a disaster and a catastrophe on the line...

The two Leeds-bound engines had departed and the only locos in the station were the two coupled Carlisle engines standing patiently on the down-line. They began to move out of the station yard and make their way northwards, into the damp night.

The midnight sleeping-car express to Glasgow roared through the station. Double-headed, and making up for lost time, its two engines laboured hard to give a good account of themselves before the gradient steepened. In the two light engines, drivers Scott and Bath had no doubts nor misgivings about their precarious position.

As far as Scott was concerned, he had been given the signal to leave Hawes Junction. Running at approximately 25 miles an hour, the two engines passed through Moorcock Tunnel and emerged into the dawn of a dreary day. Driver Bath, on the rear engine, was in good spirits. Newly promoted to driver, he was proud of his achievements with the company.

Leaning from the engine, he took stock of the early morning chill and gave a casual glance at the track and the rear of his engine. His heart gave a sudden jump, and he blinked to make sure he wasn't seeing things. Bursting forth from the entrance of Moorcock Tunnel came the unmistakable shape of an express passenger locomotive...

Back at Garsdale, Driver Tempest - a witness to the signalling fault - confronted Sutton, who was a conscientious, hard-working man. When inquiries were made, and the signalman who was to relieve him, entered the box, Sutton said, limply: "Go to the stationmaster's office, and tell him ...tell him I'm afraid I've wrecked the Scottish express."

Ken Leak (1993)

A Christmas Getaway

Have you ever thought of escaping from Christmas? It is the time of year when the country turns into a madhouse and we all become zombies.

On December 24, we packed the car with food and other essentials and set off for Robin Hood's Bay. The day was cold but fine. We drove over the North York Moors in fading afternoon light and arrived in time for tea. In the half-dark, it was difficult to find the way to our cottage through a maze of little streets.

Inside it was snug and warm and very comfortably furnished. From bedroom windows we had views of the sea spreading out below us. That evening we visited the Bay Hotel, built by the sea's edge. Sitting at the far end of the room, seeing nothing but ocean through the porthole windows, we imagined ourselves

far out to sea.

Christmas morning was lazy. We opened presents, not able to abandon tradition completely, and prepared the evening meal. In the afternoon we walked along the beach. The evening meal was a delightfully cooked joint of pork followed by chocolate mousse. We ate by candlelight and got pleasantly drunk.

By Boxing Day, the wind was raging, the sea white and angry. But we decided to brave the elements and walked the length of the beach to Raven Hall Hotel, perched on the edge of the cliff... The wind howled and, as we climbed unsteadily to the top, we had to hang on tightly to our hats. Safe inside the hotel, we wolfed down sandwiches and sipped lagers before returning home.

The next day we visited Whitby, which never fails to interest and excite. The smell of fish hangs in the damp, salty air. The gulls scream... It is easy to imagine the hard and dangerous lives of smugglers and fishermen, the distress and bereavement experienced by their wives and families.

We explored pokey, cobbled streets, ate mussels and wandered over the wide sandy beach. As evening fell, we walked along the pier. A rich, red sunset spread across the sky. The coastline and the houses on the cliffs grew darker and darker until they were black silhouettes.

We sighed with regret but also with pleasure as we realised this was the last day of our Christmas getaway to one of the most memorable and least spoiled parts of England.

Belinda Barber (1993)

A Salting of Snow

The farmer said,
Just a salting of snow -
an odd way of putting it
for salt and snow we usually see
in the mess of busy streets.

But it was aptly right
with the fawn haunches of the Howgills
spread with the salt-snow
and nicely grilling in a winter sun
set at a low number.

We raised the dust of it
as we tramped white fells
the short day through.
Just a salting of snow,
but enough to flavour

*the day so the ordinary
turned into a feast.*

Hamish Brown (1985)

Christmas at Nunnington

A log fire burns in The Stone Hall at Nunnington - in this old manor house by the river Rye near Helmsley. Fingers of light from the crackling logs compete for attention with the glow from a Christmas tree. Light falls on the skins and mounted heads of animals from the plains of Africa and the jungles of India - beasts shot by Col. Fife, of Nunnington Hall, who spent much of his time abroad.

Nunnington is now owned by the National Trust. The fire and the illuminated tree will be a features of a pre-Christmas event, when supporters of the Trust who live in the vicinity of Nunnington will muster in the Stone Hall to buy gifts at a Concert of Words and Music, the singers being drawn from York choirs.

History does not relate what the weather was like at Christmas 1702, when the Royal gardener, Monsieur Beaumont, was a guest at Nunnington Hall. Fog gathers in the Vale of York and spills over the ridge into Ryedale. Sometimes, fog is so thick you can taste it! The first appreciable snowfalls occur after Christmas.

When the day's visitors have departed, the administrator and her husband can settle down in their private quarters to celebrate Christmas, leaving the main part of the hall to the creaks and the resident ghost - a lady who climbs the stairs to a room from which her child is said to have fallen through a window to his death on the ground far below.

Winter is not a relaxing time at Nunnington Hall. Maintenance work is carried out and the place is thoroughly cleaned, from the spacious attics to the ground floor. The floor of the Stone Hall is composed of flagstones which were put in place almost 400 years ago; they have been polished by many feet into a tile-like smoothness.

W R Mitchell (1986)

Postman's Knock

For farmers with stock, Christmas Day is still a hard-working day but for most people it is a holiday. Back in the 1920s, when I was a teenager, a lot of people had to work before they got their Christmas dinner.

One of them I will always remember was our postman, Jack Horner from Hawes. In those days, the Christmas mail came at Christmas, not like today, with all this emphasis on "Post Early". This year, mine started arriving in November.

Christmas 1926 was definitely a white one. It had been snowing all night so Jack, who was a big hefty man, could not use his bike and had to set off on his round carrying his sack. They did not have vans in those days.

He might not have had many houses, but it was a long way between them - 16 miles or more there and back to deliver the mail.

He would start at Collier Holme, if not before; then it was across the fields to Mossdale before getting back to the main road at Thwaite Bridge. He then

went up to Moorland and Moorcock. After that, it was round more farms before he got to our farm at West End.

It had been snowing all day. Now it was 6pm and dark. Our menfolk had done the farming chores for the night. I had fed the hens and dogs, got in coals and peat and buckets of water for use overnight indoors. (No tap water until 1932). Mother had been busy indoors. The parlour fire had been on all day, the lamp was lit and the big dining table was loaded with food, including a Christmas cake which I had iced.

There were nine of us to sit around the table. Baby Harold was in the cradle. Suddenly, there was a loud rat-a-tat-tat on the outdoor and we were all startled. Father said: "Who on earth is out at 6pm on Christmas Day?" We hadn't expected a visit from the postman on such an awful day and so father shouted to me as I opened the door: "Who is it?" I told him.

Jack was invited in for some tea. He doffed his snowy overcoat and settled down, enjoying a Christmas tea and a good chat with the Scarr family. That over, he got geared up and went away across the fell bottom to White Birch, with more mail. Presumably he would brew up again in the Postman's Hut at Moorcock and then set off to trek back to Hawes and home.

At the market on the following Tuesday, we heard that he arrived home in the small hours of Boxing Day. Mrs Horner and their son, Lou, would not have had a very happy time, wondering where he was on such a wintry day. It was a thrill, though, for us to have someone unexpected to stay for Christmas tea. This is one of those things which has been mentioned in our family almost every Christmas since.

Alice Dinsdale (1993).

A Kessemas Wish

Here's ti thoo, an' all 'at's thahn,
Here's ti me, an' all 'at's mahn.
Maay all t'gopod luck, 'at luck can send,
Be thahn an' mahn reeght up ti t'end
Is what Ah wish, an' what Ah pray
Ti leeght on all this Kessemas Daay.

Old Yorkshire Saying

Santa in a Spin

The Malton Lions Club had hired Hovingham Village Hall to give a Christmas party to a group of children gathered from an area between York and Scarborough. Getting the children to Hovingham had been a nightmare in itself. Not only had the area been blanketed in freezing fog for over a week but we had the "winter mud" probably worse than ever this year. Somehow we all made it through the fog to Hovingham.

The children trooped uncertainly into the hall to be met by our eager volunteers, who took their coats and explained about the games we had selected to suit the restricted abilities of our guests. We need not have worried about play problems. The kids had no problems, but we had. Games that took ages to explain to adults were accepted with glee by the children in seconds. Soon, bean bags were flying in all directions.

After the games came food, lots of it, plus pop and ice cream. The magician did his bit. The grand finale was to be Father Christmas. In the

"You can't make a good Christmas dinner better by serving it in fancy dishes".

famous sack was a carefully selected present for each child. One of our members had volunteered to be Father Christmas and had disappeared discreetly into the Young Farmers' room behind the stage when the cakes and pop had been eaten and the magician was about to begin.

The plan was for the magician to do his 30 minutes, by which time Father Christmas, in hood and whiskers, would come quietly round behind the curtains at the side of the stage as a signal to the magician to produce the white rabbit and bring his act to a close.

There was no Father Christmas. I went in search of him. He had slammed the door of the Young Farmers' room behind him and, the handle coming away, he was unable to open it again. The figure before me was near to collapse. He had aged several years in the past hour. Heaven knows what his blood pressure was at that moment.

It took several minutes to calm him down and re-arrange his whiskers and costume before we crept back into the hall. The magician, visibly relieved, produced the white rabbit. Loud acclaim followed. He bowed and departed for a much needed drink in the Malt Shovel next door.

Father Christmas entered. He was still trembling. The children gave squeals of delight. Soon every child had been given a present. The floor was covered with colour wrapping paper and new toys were being displayed and compared all round the hall. The cars crept out into the night, returning the children to their homes.

Back in the hall, I found a figure slumped on a chair in a corner. At his feet was a carrier bag containing shiny black Wellingtons, a red robe and white whiskers of soggy cotton wool. "Never again," croaked Father Christmas. "Never again..."

Derek Low (1993)

A Dales Christmas

A Wensleydale farmer told me: "They didn't mak' so much fuss about Christmas in t'awd days." There was a time for reverence, a time for good eating ("aye, it wor days afore a man's ribs settled into place") and a time for hard work. You can't tak time off on a farm."

A woman in the same dale did not remember Christmas trees as such. "In our house, mother went out and gathered some greens. She made them into a bundle which she drooped from a hook set in the kitchen ceiling. On Christmas Day, we had oranges and apples and a few tinsel things - nothing expensive, mind you. But there was such a lovely fragrant smell from the evergreens."

At Malham, a farmer's wife realised on Christmas Day there was no tree, so she went out with the family and they cut down a small conifer. There was still rime on the branches when it was placed in a tub in the living room. The woman went out to milk her stock - by hand. As she milked, one of the children ran out and said the Christmas tree had caught fire.

The distraught woman set off to run into the house. Her daughter said: "You don't need to go in just yet. The fire's out." When asked how she had put it out, she replied: "I threw a jugful of milk over it." The house reeked of burnt milk for days.

Christmas gifts? In Wharfedale, "you got an orange

and an apple, and a few nuts, and a sugar pig. You pretended you were killing a proper pig, and got a knife out of t'drawer to have a butchering day, cutting up the pig! I also remembered getting some painted icing sugar, one piece being shaped like a mouse, wi' a bit o' wool for its tail."

Christmas food included a goose or a roast of pork and "generally some boiled ham." Plum pudding, or barley pudding - "it was just made of barley" - might be served. Frumenty was served at Reeth, in Swaledale, and "men wi' blackened faces and fancy costumes knocked at the house doors and asked if they could enter and sing."

A modern Christmas is remembered for its excesses, with too much food and too much synthetic entertainment in over-heated rooms.

Dalesman (1982).

Winter by the Derwent

The annual flooding of the Derwent valley, below York, is spectacular. For several months one has been aware of an overall greenness. Almost overnight the waters spread and by December there is the gunmetal-grey of the extensive floods.

In a normal winter, between 120 and 200 Bewick's swans are present. They stay right through a freeze-up, for if the Ings are solid ice the birds go on to the river to feed. Birdwatchers who clump across the Bailey bridge follow a path beside the Derwent, which is running almost bank high, deep and brown, swirling like porridge in a pan.

From a hide beside the river, the visiting naturalist has a wide view of the massed birds. Wigeon swirl in the sky. The floodwater holds large parties of mallard and teal. On the sodden fringes are waders, golden plover and lapwing among them. The water birds are eating the rhizomes of marsh plants, particularly reed grass and iris. They also take the seeds of plants.

A native of these parts I met at Yew Tree Farm, Thorganby, told me that in the old days when ice formed on the flooded land in winter, "50 or 60 kiddies from the village, with stable lamps, would be down there skating. They could all jump together on the ice without cracking it." Yew Tree Farm is close enough to the Ings for the inhabitants to hear the cracking of ice at the time of the thaw. "It echoes up the valley".

W R Mitchell (1987)

THE NORTH'S LEADING PUBLISHER
FOR MORE THAN 40 YEARS

Here is a selection of other books that may interest you:

THE DALESMAN BEDSIDE BOOK
(ISBN 1 85568 065 3)
YORKSHIRE'S CHRISTMAS
(ISBN 1 85568 050 5)
YORKSHIRE DALES STONEWALLER
(ISBN 1 85568 049 1)
YORKSHIRE LEGENDS
(ISBN 1 85568 067 X)
TALES FROM THE DALESMAN
(ISBN 1 85568 068 8)
BEST YORKSHIRE TALES
(ISBN 1 85568 030 0)

With over 150 books to choose from the Dalesman range
covers subjects as diverse as:
WALKING, WILDLIFE, HUMOUR, TOPOGRAPHY,
ANTHOLOGIES, HOLIDAY GUIDES, GHOSTS AND
SPORT

For a catalogue of all the Dalesman titles send a SAE to:
DALESMAN PUBLISHING CO LTD
CLAPHAM, VIA LANCASTER, LA2 8EB